Breath of GOD

Devotions and Prayers for
Experiencing the Life of God

JONI BANKS

Breath of God: Devotions and Prayers for Experiencing the Life of God
Copyright © 2018 by Joni Banks
Published by 5 Fold Media, LLC
www.5foldmedia.com

All rights reserved. No part of this book may be reproduced, stored in a retrieval system, or transmitted in any form or by any means—electronic, mechanical, photocopy, recording, or otherwise-without prior written permission of the copyright owner. The views and opinions expressed from the writer are not necessarily those of 5 Fold Media, LLC.

Unless otherwise noted, all Scripture quotations are taken from the Amplified® Bible, copyright © 1954, 1958, 1962, 1964, 1965, 1987 by The Lockman Foundation. Used by permission.

Scriptures marked JB are taken from *The Jerusalem Bible* © 1966 by Darton Longman & Todd Ltd and Doubleday and Company Ltd.

Scripture quotations marked (NLT) are taken from the Holy Bible, New Living Translation, copyright © 1996, 2004, 2007, 2013, 2015 by Tyndale House Foundation. Used by permission of Tyndale House Publishers, Inc., Carol Stream, Illinois 60188. All rights reserved.

Scripture quotations marked AMP are taken from the Amplified® Bible, Copyright © 2015 by The Lockman Foundation. Used by permission.

Photography for Author's picture by Michelle Daily Rinkey, Rinkey's Photography.

ISBN: 978-1-942056-65-2

Library of Congress Control Number: 2018933449

Printed in the USA

I lovingly dedicate this book to my children. It is my legacy to you, your children, and future generations, should the Lord tarry. My prayer of all prayers is that one day, because of the precious blood of Jesus, we will enjoy eternity together in heaven.

Acknowledgments

To my friend, Marcia Todd, the one who took the time to proofread this writing. Thank you for your prayers, encouraging words, and honesty. You did much more than merely proofread what I wrote. You inspired a passion in me to complete what began as a deep heart cry to leave a godly legacy to my children, grandchildren, and future generations.

Thank you...

To my heavenly Father, the One who gave me breath. In your mercy, You lifted me out of the ashes of sin and failure. Your love and forgiveness have filled my life with hope and beauty.

Thank you...

To my husband and dearest friend, Steven. Your love and faithfulness have given me wings to fly like a butterfly with the dreams in my heart.

Thank you...

To my godly mother who never ceases to pray for her children and grandchildren. Your prayers and petitions rise to the Father as beautiful, powerful beams of light. We will never know 'til we reach heaven what your love and prayers have accomplished.

Breath of God

Thank you...

To my dad up in heaven. I can feel your love and encouragement even from here to fulfill every dream in my heart and reach my destiny in the Lord.

Thank you...

To my brothers and sisters. You know better than anyone my every wart and flaw! We grew up together. What else can I say? I feel your eternal acceptance and love because we're more than just friends; we're family. We are forever joined in the bloodline of our earthly parents, but more importantly, the blood of Jesus Christ.

Thank you...

To our precious children. Your love means the world to us. We cannot begin to express what we feel in our hearts for each of you. Your smiles light up our lives. I wrote this book with you in my heart. I believe in you. Run the race. Reach for the stars. May nothing distract you from your ultimate destiny—heaven. The greatest goal of all is to know your Creator intimately. Everything else in your life will supernaturally fall into place as you seek Him with all your heart. Thank you for the beautiful gift you gave us in our grandchildren. They are pure delight to our hearts. Their smiles, hugs, and laughter flood our home with joy.

Thank you...

A huge thank you to our ministry covering pastors, Darrell and Marcia Todd; our fellow minister, Pastor

Marie Hanson; and to our precious brothers and sisters at Fountain of Hope Ministries. Your prayers, faithfulness, love, friendship, and support have been so integral in our lives and ministry. Thank you for loving us and believing in the heart of what God has called us to do in this ministry—love.

Contents

Foreword	11
If Breath Had a Language	13
Stillness	15
Veiled Glory	17
Habitation	21
Deeper	23
Zoe	25
Breathless	27
The Priceless Treasure	29
Breathe Him In	31
More Costly Than Gold	33
God's Masterpiece	35
God's Glory Revealed	37
Your First Breath	39
This Water Is Alive	41
Eyes Flooded with Light	43
The Ultimate Teacher	47
Angels Among Us	49
An Angel Story	51
The Explosive Power of Prayer	53
Show Me Your Glory	57
The Battlefield	59
Breathe His Name	63
It's Your Breath in My Lungs	65
In Spirit and in Truth	67
Fresh Bread from Heaven	69

Breath of God

God Dances over You	73
Beauty for Ashes	75
Fresh Oil	77
Supernatural Provision	81
The Master Goldsmith	85
The Garments of Praise	87
God-Breathed Dreams	89
Inhale, Exhale	91
Our Eternal Home	93
Closer	95
Breathe in His Word	97
The Names of God	99
The Main Thing	103
Dry Bones Come Alive	105
Jesus' Final Breath	107

Foreword

I first met Joni at a little town hall tucked away in a rural community in northeastern Minnesota. It wasn't the sort of place you got to by accident, unless one was lost and wandering. We were neither. A mutual heartfelt cry to see God move brought us to the little town hall that chilly, winter night. It was surely no accident.

Since meeting Joni for the very first time more than two decades ago, her love for the Lord is obvious. She loves her family, friends, and the gathering of believers as they come to worship; most of all, she just loves Him. Her heart's cry is to know Jesus, to be more like Him, and to see others fall in love with the Lover of her soul. It is not something she just talks about. She lives it, and it can be experienced when you are with her.

As I read the first pages of her book, I was supposed to be proofreading. I began reading, pencil in hand, ready to read critically and make notes of what I found. I started to read and came to my senses when I was done. I had not written a thing. My heart was fixed upon her words, and I had just had an encounter with Jesus.

When she first told me why she was writing a book, it was to have a tangible way to express and impart her love of her Lord that could be shared with family for generations. She wanted them to know her heart and experience for themselves the God who has breathed His life into her as she has lived her life here on earth. As you hold this book in your hands, you get to share in all she wishes to impart to those she loves. Knowing Joni as I do, she loves you, too.

I invite you to open the pages of this book, to read the words written in it, and to listen with your heart. Take a deep breath and ask God to breathe His life into you as you read and experience what is contained in these pages. You may never be the same.

—Marcia Todd
Pastor and Co-Founder of Word and Sound Ministries

If Breath Had a Language

**Psalms 34:1-5 | Acts 17:28 | Jeremiah 18:1-6
Psalms 27:8 | 2 Corinthians 3:18**

Breath of God, You put breath in my lungs to praise You.

Breath. How vital to our very existence on this planet. When God formed Adam from the dust of the ground, the Bible says in Genesis 2:7, "[He] breathed into his nostrils the breath of life; and the man became a living being." Until God breathed into that pile of dirt, it was a mere shell of a man. It could not move, see, hear, or feel. It was just that—a pile of dirt. The all-powerful Creator, God, turned a pile of dirt into a living, breathing, eternal soul.

As we breathe, we are doing much more than just taking in oxygen and releasing carbon dioxide. We are declaring the very existence of God. If our breath had a language, with each inhale I believe it whispers, "Yahweh, Life-Giver," and with each exhale, "Yahweh, Life-Sustainer."

Breath of God

Prayer:

Precious heavenly Father, in the quiet of this moment I ask that You would come and breathe Your breath of life afresh into the depths of my being. Come and blow Your warm, regenerating winds through me, that every cell in my body will rise up and praise You. With every breath I take, I will declare that You are the only one worthy of my worship. I worship Your majesty and Your greatness. I worship You because of who You are—Yahweh, Life-Giver and Life-Sustainer. I invite the transforming power of Your presence to change me more and more into Your likeness. As I look to You, I am radiant. Holy Potter of this piece of clay, make me, mold me, shape me into a vessel of honor for Your glory. My earnest prayer this day is that I may be so consumed and infiltrated by Your Holy Spirit that it will be evident to all that I have been with You, Jesus.

Stillness

**Psalms 46:10 | Psalms 25:14
Isaiah 26:3 | Psalm 91**

Breath of God, I wait for You.

Breathe deeply. Breathe in His presence. Tune out the noise of the world, and with your spiritual ears tune in to the sound of heaven. Draw on the strength of God and tell your anxious mind, "Be still."

As you do this, every other voice is overshadowed by the one voice that matters—God's. Listen closely. Sense the wind of His Spirit breathing His perfect peace into your mind. Lay hold of this moment and draw close. This is where you belong physically, emotionally, and spiritually. You belong in God's sacred garden of serenity. Here you will experience renewed, supernatural strength infused into the very depths of your being.

Determine today to make His priorities your priorities. Your destiny is discovered in the secret place. The deepest secrets of God's heart are revealed here. This is the highest honor of those He calls His very own. Enjoy truly living today.

Prayer:

Oh, Jesus, You are my shalom, my peace. I quiet my soul before You now and wait. I am listening for the sound of Your voice. Please, open my spiritual ears and my spiritual eyes that I may hear Your voice and see Your face. I long for more of You. In this quiet moment, I drink deeply of Your river of peace. As a drowning man is desperate for air, I am desperate for Your holy, refreshing breath in my lungs. Speak, Lord; I'm waiting. I'm listening for Your still, small voice to come and thunder in the depths of my being.

Veiled Glory

**John 3:15-17 | Philippians 2:9
Isaiah 9:1-7 | 1 Corinthians 13**

Breath of God, breathe upon me a deeper
revelation of Your divine plan.

There was no other way. Adam and Eve had relinquished their authority to that deceiver snake, the Devil. They were now banished from their heaven on earth, forever. Their downfall? It was the lust to be gods and possess the knowledge that belongs to God alone. The first human beings blew it. Oh, the anguish, the shame, and the heartache that must have enveloped them when their eyes were suddenly opened. Plan A was now rendered null and void.

God knew this would happen and was already prepared with Plan B. It wasn't going to be easy, but love never takes the easy route, does it? To reconcile His creation back to Himself, a perfect blood sacrifice would be necessary. Not even one cell could be tainted. Absolute perfection was required. If left undone, eternal separation was imminent. Plan B was about to unfold.

Thus, the love story of all love stories unfolds, consisting of a young, unmarried teenager; a crushed, bewildered

Breath of God

fiancé; and a Baby. It sounds more like a scandal than a divine plan. The very shekinah glory of God makes His entrance on planet earth veiled in skin and rags. With His first cry, He breathed the odor of dung and hay dust. Veiled in the flesh of a newborn child lay Emmanuel, the Savior of all mankind. Where was the golden cradle, the blankets of silk, the palace, and the silver spoon? The Hero of all humanity has arrived. Our humble King Jesus is here. Hope is alive.

Prayer:

Oh Jesus, Lamb of God, I am so grateful and humbled to be the object of Your love. I have failed You miserably so many times. I've broken Your heart in a million pieces, yet You did not abandon me. Your love has brought me back from the dead. You are my story of hope. You could have called myriads of angels to rescue You and wipe out all humanity in the process. It is inconceivable to me that You didn't. Thank You, Jesus, that the power of Your blood breaks every chain of darkness that would imprison me. Like a bird let out of its cage, I am free. May my every breath release a fresh expression of my love for You. I long for the day I encounter You face to face and perfected praise resounds from my heart to Yours for all eternity.

"Let everything that has breath and every breath of life *praise the Lord!*" (Psalms 150:6)

Habitation

**Ephesians 2:19-22 (KJV) | Acts 17:24-25
2 Corinthians 6:16-18 | Psalm 16**

Breath of God, breathe upon me a holy desire to draw closer to You than ever before.

As the hour draws near for Jesus' return, holy intimacy between Jesus and His bride will become more and more passionate. Holy habitation will mark His true sons and daughters in this final season. A deep longing for His presence will flood the hearts of His true worshipers. Unhindered, undignified, and passionate worship will spontaneously arise to the Lover of our soul from every nation of the world.

God is breathing a desire for deeper intimacy into His chosen ones. Listen as He speaks with love to His Bride, "Come away with Me to the secret mountain of holiness, My child, where we may enjoy the sweetest of communion together. Come, discover the rivers of pleasure in My presence."

Prayer:

Precious Jesus, I fix my gaze upon You. I look to You, and I am radiant and at peace. Thank You that because of Your precious blood I may enter the secret chamber of Your Holy presence. I worship You in the beauty of holiness. I feast at the table of Your goodness. I quietly sit at Your feet and receive strength and fresh revelation from Your heart. This is where I was always meant to be. I'm home when I'm with You.

Deeper

Genesis 5:22-24 | Psalms 27:4 | Psalm 145

Breath of God, breathe in me a deeper manifestation of who You are.

Deeper, deeper every day. As we seek the face of our Father God, more and more of His nature unfolds. The love in His eyes will leave us breathless. We were never meant to be satisfied knowing our Creator from afar. He longs to be discovered in fresh, new ways continually by His beloved. As a groom lifts the veil of his bride on their wedding day, the Father lifts the veil from our spiritual eyes, revealing more and more of Himself to us as we seek Him with all our heart.

Through all eternity, there will be more and more of His love and character to unveil. He has secrets to reveal to His bride, divine destiny to unwrap. Breakthroughs arise out of difficult places. Trust leaps off the charts. Fears are vanquished as we look into His eyes. Limitless revelation of who He is awaits those who passionately require His presence more than riches, more than food, and more than breath.

Prayer:

Dear heavenly Father, You are the eternal, unsearchable, uncreated, indescribable One. Today I ask for a fresh manifestation of who You are. Unveil my eyes to envision You in a way I have never known before. Forgive me for anything that would hinder intimate access to the secrets of Your heart. Loose my finite mind that I may reach new heights in my quest for Your presence. I adore You. I'm waiting for You. I am listening. Your voice is the voice I need to hear. I long to hear Your heartbeat as we walk together, hand in hand, through this life. Let the weight of Your glory fall on me.

Zoe

**Matthew 7:14 | John 1:4
John 10:10 | Matthew 1:23**

Breath of God, breathe in me Your zoe life.

No one wants to merely exist. We all have a deep desire to experience life to the fullest and know our existence has purpose.

Zoe is a Greek word that means life—the God kind of life. Strong's concordance describes *zoe* as being "life, real and genuine, a life active and vigorous, devoted to God, blessed, even in this world for those who put their trust in Christ…and to last forever."

This is the life you were always meant to live. Anything less will leave within you a gnawing emptiness. No amount of money, material things, or fame will even come close to the fulfillment found in the zoe life of God. As you feast on God's love letter, the Bible, the zoe life of God is infused into the very depths of your being. You can trust that no matter what this day may bring, you are not alone. Every worry and fear will vanish in the light of God's zoe life. God will supernaturally carry you through each moment in His boundless, infinite love.

Breath of God

God the Father gave Jesus the name *Emmanuel*, which means "God with us." Over 2,000 years later, He still wants to be with you. God longs to breathe His breath of life into you. Inhale deeply and experience the zoe life of God. He is the omniscient, all-knowing One with all the answers, so ask His advice on everything. A life signed with the signature of God is the life of one who has truly lived.

Prayer:

Father God, You are the Author of life. You are the only One worthy of my praise. I honor You. I exalt You. I enter Your gates with thanksgiving. Thank You for life and for including me in Your grand design. I want to experience the life You have planned for me. As I am quiet in Your presence, breathe Your life in me. Come with Your refreshing, healing wind and restore my life from the inside out. As one searches for costly treasure, I seek for You. Here is my life, Lord. I offer it up to You as a living sacrifice. Your presence is the one thing I never want to be without. The world has left me so empty and lifeless. You are my vital need. Fill me, Jesus; fill me with Your zoe life now and forever.

Breathless

John 3

Breath of God, Your love takes my breath away.

Clear your mind of everything else, and allow your heart to ponder God's unconditional love for you. His love will leave you breathless. You are the object of God's love. God is love, and love is from God. You are the apple of His eye. In the midst of all your inadequacies, the Father looks upon you tenderly and pours out His perfect love. God loves you with an everlasting love. As a father guards and protects his child, God is your defender.

The demands of life can be extremely draining. They can cause you to lose sight of the love of God. This can open your spirit to a feeling of being overwhelmed and downcast. It breaks the Father's heart to see your heart weighed down with burdens and cares. He waits to softly whisper words such as these into the depths of your soul:

"My child, I see your heart of hearts. Lift your face to Me. Gaze into My eyes of love. I see your hands that hang down. Raise them up to Me. I will gather you in My arms and hold you with My healing embrace.

"Let every care float away, and dance like a child in the refreshing rain of My love. Live in the embrace of heaven. Feel the holy kiss of My love, for My love is all you will ever need."

Prayer:

Oh, Father, I want to thank You today for Your boundless love. As I meditate now on Your great love, let Your love wash over me. You created me with the vital need to experience Your love.

Thank You that as I fill my mind with Your Word, You release in me Your love, Your thoughts, Your mind, and Your will. You are the very air I breathe.

Leave me breathless today, Father, with a fresh revelation of Your love.

The Priceless Treasure

**2 Corinthians 4:6-12 | Hebrews 12:1-3
1 Peter 2:4-9**

Breath of God, breathe in me a fresh
revelation of the treasure of Your presence
living in me.

Picture finding the most exquisite, perfectly cut diamond or luminescent pearl wrapped in a brown paper bag with a bow made of plain, jute twine. This is what I envision when I think of God living inside of these earthen vessels. Deity—the Holy Spirit—residing in clay.

It can be very difficult for the human brain to wrap itself around this. It is spiritually discerned. Ask the Holy Spirit to fill you today with fresh revelation of this astounding truth. It will transform even the most dismal of days into one filled with the zoe life of God.

Today, do a one-eighty in the Spirit. The treasure of all treasures, the Holy Spirit, has chosen to reside inside of you. This is the day the Lord has made. Rejoice in the beauty you will discover in this day.

Breath of God

Prayer:

Gracious Father, I want to express my deepest gratitude for choosing to live inside of me. I know I do not deserve the treasure of Your Holy Spirit, but oh, how I appreciate Your presence in me. You are breath and life to me. I need You more than air.

Your presence fills me with courage and strengthens me when I'm tempted to abandon the call. You make me fearless and brave. You obliterate every area of selfishness in me and replace it with a generous, selfless heart.

Thank You that each passing day I am being transformed more and more into Your image. Yesterday is gone, supernaturally forgiven and forgotten, and buried in the deepest sea. I leave it there.

Your mercies are new every morning. It's a new day. I'm running toward the prize of the high calling of God in my life.

Breathe Him In

2 Timothy 3:16-17 | Job 32:8
Psalms 33:6 | Job 33:4

Breath of God, almighty God, right now I take this moment to deeply breathe in Your presence.

Breathe Him in. Only Him. Allow God alone to permeate your being. This is where you belong, in the green pastures of God. It is here that His peace replaces all fear, anxiety, and lies of the Devil.

It is in this place where everything changes. Divine destiny unfolds. The to-do list suddenly seems do-able and not so burdensome as God lovingly erases some things and adds in His divine appointments. Each day, you will continually, supernaturally have enough time and strength to accomplish His plan. Just breathe.

Breathe deeply from the Source of life. Enjoy that place of total dependence on your heavenly Father. The joy of the Lord is your strength.

Prayer:

Gracious Father, I worship You. I adore You. I depend upon You for my very breath. It is Your hand that has given me food, clothing, shelter, and every blessing I enjoy in this life. I am not my own. I belong to You. I invite You now to breathe into me Your plan for this day. Come, Lord, take the pen and write. I want to store up treasures in Heaven where nothing can destroy them. Use me to sow into someone's life with eternal seeds. As long as I have breath, may Your Kingdom come and Your will be done in my life.

More Costly Than Gold

**Job 22:21-30 | Matthew 6:24-34
1 Timothy 6:10 | Deuteronomy 8:17-18**

Breath of God, give me the grace to choose
Your presence over any earthly treasure.

Job 22:24-25 says, "If you lay gold in the dust, and the gold of Ophir among the stones of the brook [considering them of little worth], and make the Almighty your gold and [the Lord] your precious silver."

God owns it all. It blesses Him when we choose His presence over anything created. When we have His Word hidden in our hearts, we have the power to choose His presence over anything created. There truly is no comparison when it comes to earthly riches or His presence. God's presence is priceless.

The end of a little joke I've heard places a man in heaven standing before St. Peter, carrying a suitcase full of gold. St. Peter asks the man why he has lugged pavement into heaven. Revelation 21:21 says the streets of heaven are paved with gold. What he had considered so important while on earth was really just sidewalk material.

Breath of God

Lay up treasures in heaven, dear one, where neither moth nor rust can corrupt it. Heavenly treasure lasts forever.

Prayer:

Forgive me, Father, for the times I have made riches my priority over Your presence. I commit today that Your presence is the gold I will seek after. Your presence is what I run after. Help me to see riches as an instrument in Your hands to use as You see fit. I worship You only, Father. I lay the gold of riches in the dust. I will not idolize anything created, for You alone are worthy of my worship. I want to store up treasures in heaven—the treasure of souls. I love You.

God's Masterpiece

Psalm 8 | Ephesians 2:10 (NLT)
Jeremiah 29:11-13 | Ecclesiastes 3:10-11

Breath of God, You are the Master Artisan.

Psalms 19:1 says, "The heavens declare the glory of God." God simply released a word, and suddenly the beauty of creation materialized. When we know our Creator, the beauty of His creation, this includes you, comes to life in vibrant, living color.

You are God's prized masterpiece. You are created in His very image. Until the Creator breathes His breath of life and purpose into us, we are mere shells. As you yield the canvas of your life to Him, God, the Master Artisan, delicately raises His creative paintbrush and begins to paint. Stroke by stroke, with exquisite intricacy, He paints you.

The masterpiece of who you were always meant to be begins to take shape. Your destiny unfolds in wave after wave of complete uniqueness. The fingerprints of God appear all over you and your purpose.

When God finally sets His paintbrush down and the picture of your life is complete, it will be far more than you could have ever imagined.

Breath of God

Ah, but there remains yet one final step. The signature—the signature of God. The Master Artist takes His pen and lovingly signs His autograph. Unashamed, He lifts the veil and reveals to the world, "Behold My masterpiece, the work of My hands." You.

Prayer:

Gracious Father, thank You for the plan You have foreordained for my life. I know Your plan will bring fulfillment to my life. I give all that I am to You. You are the Potter. I am the clay. I give You the canvas of my life. Transform it into something beautiful in Your eyes.

Breathe Your breath of life into the purpose of my existence. I know You will not leave me ashamed or disappointed. You're a good, good Father. I love You.

Paint away, Father. I'm ready.

God's Glory Revealed

**Psalms 19:1-6 | Exodus 33:18-23
Isaiah 40:5 | Hebrews 1:3**

Breath of God, let me see Your glory.

Envision the beauty of majestic mountains, a blazing orange sunset, and the vastness of the Grand Canyon. These are but a few examples of the magnificent sights God has created with us in mind. As we close our eyes, we can relive these beautiful scenes again and again with our mind's eye. It was for more than our viewing pleasure alone that He made all of this. He painted each detail to declare to us His magnificent glory. Though it never speaks a word, God shouts through His creation, "Behold My handiwork! I am here. I made all of this for you! I love you."

Creation displays undeniable evidence that there is a God.

The heavens are talking continually. Are we listening?

Prayer:

Holy God, Creator of all, I am so in awe of You. Only You could produce such magnificent splendor. It is delightful to behold. As I ponder the vastness of the universe, one word comes to mind—indescribable. My finite mind cannot comprehend Your creative power and Your magnitude.

You manifest Your presence in the cool refreshing breeze, the warmth of the sun, and the flowers and trees along my journey. You made heaven and earth, and yet You see me and hear me in this little room. I feel Your love in this place. I am on holy ground.

Precious Holy Spirit, help me to hear You speaking today through Your creation.

Your First Breath

Ecclesiastes 3:1-2 | Job 33:4 | John 3:5-8

Breath of God, You breathed Your breath of life in me for a purpose.

At birth, you drew your first breath of air. What a sacred, miraculous, God-ordained moment. With that first cry, a process was set into motion that will continue throughout your lifetime. Though you cannot see it, smell it, feel it, or taste it, air is most vital to your existence.

It is not by chance you took your first breath. It is not by chance that you are breathing now. God wants to breathe the supernatural breath of His Spirit into you this moment, and the next, and the next.

His presence is a beautiful gift. Breathe in the life-giving breath of God. His breath will fill your life with purpose. His breath will saturate you with joy in difficult places. His breath will release the dance of a child within you. He delights to see His children dance for joy in His presence.

Be awed and humbled in the presence of the Life-Giver.

Breath of God

Prayer:

Gracious heavenly Father, thank You for the breath of life. With each breath, may grateful praise rise out of the depths of my heart to Yours. I adore You. I breathe for You. By the blood of Your Son Jesus, I enter Your presence. Please, forgive me for using my breath for anything less than praise. I bow my knees before You, in awe of who You are. You have captured my heart with Your love.

I am born again in Your presence. Come and breathe the breath of Your Spirit into my lungs.

This Water Is Alive

John 4:14 | Psalms 65:9 | Isaiah 55:1-13

Breath of God, refresh me today with Your springs of living water.

The most soothing, peaceful, and therapeutic moments I've experienced in this life have been while sitting by the ocean, early in the morning, with a cup of coffee and my Bible in hand. As I gaze at the magnificence before me and read the words written by the One who created it all, total renewal takes place inside me. Watching the waves washing up on the shore, one after the other, reminds me of waves of the Holy Spirit washing over me. With the crashing of each wave, the debris of this world is removed from my soul and replaced with God's refreshing, reviving water. I could sit for hours, taking in the breathtaking beauty and saturating my soul in the living water of God's Word. It's like the Creator and creation colliding afresh and anew for the very first time, again.

This supernatural, life-giving, satisfying water is free for the asking. Not even the wealthiest person on earth can afford it. It's not for sale, but it is free for the thirsty, humble heart. "Come," God says, "it's on Me. Come and drink to your heart's content."

Prayer:

Father God, Giver of life, fill me with Your refreshing water as I wait in Your presence. Living in this fallen world leaves me spiritually dehydrated. I come to You now and drink deeply of Your supernatural, living springs. Let the waves of Your presence wash over me. Let it wash away all the debris and replace it with fresh vision.

As I wait on You, I mount up with wings like an eagle. I soar closer and closer to the source of my life—You. Today, Father, I'm asking for an overflow. Let my cup run over with life-giving water so that I'm not depleted as I minister to others. I pray that Your river will continually bubble out of the overflow of Your Spirit in me.

Today, I will run and not grow weary. I will walk and not faint. Thank You for new strength in the river of Your presence.

Eyes Flooded with Light

Ephesians 1:17-23 | 1 John 1:5
Acts 9:1-10 | Psalms 97:11

Breath of God, flood the eyes of my heart
with Your light.

In our limited human understanding, the word *light* may create a picture of the warm rays of the sun we enjoy on a cloudless day. In Acts 9, Saul (now Paul) is blinded and thrown off his horse by a totally different kind of light. God gave Saul breath, but he was using that breath to breathe out cruelty and death sentences against God's people. The very light of the glory of God showed up that day. The light was so brilliant it blinded Saul for three days. God allowed just enough of His glory to overcome him so that it got his attention but didn't consume him. Why? God had a plan for this sinner.

God also has a plan for you, no matter what you have done, no matter how far you may have run from His presence. Oh, the revelation Saul received that day while wrapped in the revealing light of God. The first

Breath of God

words out of Saul's mouth? "Who are You, Lord?" There was no question in Saul's heart who he had encountered that day.

In Ephesians 1, Paul opens with a prayer for the church of Ephesus. In verse eighteen, he prays that the eyes of their hearts would be flooded with light. I believe Paul may have been reflecting on that day his eyes were flooded with God's magnificent light.

That same light also transformed John Newton, writer of the famous hymn "Amazing Grace." God's revealing light turned a slave-trader into a love-slave. "I once was lost, but now I'm found, was blind, but now I see." The true light of God will stop us right in our sinful, religious tracks and make us genuine, transparent lovers of God. Today, let's pray for the transforming light of God to flood our spiritual eyes.

Prayer:

Holy Father of light, come, I pray, and invade the eyes of my heart with Your transforming light. Unveil my eyes that I may behold Your face and be forever changed. Remove the scales from my eyes that trusting in my own understanding has caused. I want to trust You. I want to see You. I want to be like You. You, Father, are the delight of my heart. I worship You, for You alone are

God. I look to You, my source of breath, my daily bread, and my confidence.

Light my pathway so I may fulfill the purpose You have preordained for my life. I don't want to wander out on my own before Your perfect timing. Help me to follow You, step by step. Enlighten my spiritual eyes to receive fresh revelation from Your heart. Your Word is alive. Cause me to come alive as I read and meditate upon it. Be glorified in me today, I pray, in Jesus' name.

The Ultimate Teacher

John 20:19-22 | 1 Corinthians 3:16
1 Corinthians 1:26-31 | James 1:1-13

Breath of God, help me listen to the Teacher within—Your precious Holy Spirit.

Quiet your mind. Take a moment and allow your heart to ponder an awesome truth. God Himself inhabits you with His Holy Spirit. Go ahead; go there. Your body is the home of God. Let God flood the eyes of your heart with fresh revelation. With God inside of you, anything is possible.

Listen. God is talking. He has secrets to reveal to those who fear Him. As the Holy Spirit brings revelation to your heart, write it down. Your destiny is divinely wrapped between His Word and the revelation He gives.

In John 22:21-22, we read that after Jesus rose from the dead, He walked through a locked door where His disciples were gathered and supernaturally stood among them. He said, "Peace to you! [Just] as the Father has sent Me forth, so I am sending you." Then Jesus breathed on them and said, "Receive the Holy Spirit!" Jesus knew they would need the ultimate Teacher to fulfill their divine destiny. The same Holy Spirit who empowered them empowers you.

What a dynamic thought. God-moments happen when we hear the voice of the Holy Spirit and obey. Today, supernaturally go in Jesus' name, empowered by the Holy Spirit. Carry the aroma, the fragrance of Christ, everywhere you go. Take a faith-risk and touch someone. See with His eyes. Hear with His ears. Remember always who lives inside of you.

Prayer:

Right now, I quiet myself before You, Holy Spirit of God. You are the Teacher. I am Your student. Your voice is the voice I long to hear. I ask You today to open the ears and eyes of my heart. I admit that apart from You I can do nothing of eternal value. Please fill me with Your wisdom. Your Word says I have the mind of Christ. Help me to live and love like I do.

Teach me, divine Teacher, what earthly books can never teach me. I want to be a delight to Your heart. I know I will never be perfect as long as I am bound to this earth, but please help me to never grieve Your heart. May it be said of me at the end of my journey that I had my Father's eyes and loved with my Father's heart.

Angels Among Us

**Psalms 91:11-12 | Luke 22:43
Hebrews 1:14 | Mark 16:1-7**

Breath of God, thank You for assigning to us messengers, helpers, and guardians. Your angels are among us.

Our heavenly Father thought of everything. What a comforting thought that we were on His mind when He created the angels. God is constantly thinking about you. You are the apple of His eye, which means you are greatly cherished.

When Jesus arrived on earth in human form, the heavens opened up and thousands upon thousands of angels appeared. They had a huge party in the sky right in front of some lowly shepherds. I'm quite sure their jaws dropped as they watched the angels dancing for joy and shouting praises to God. What a red-letter day for those shepherds. I'm sure they passed down this story to their children and grandchildren for many generations.

Even though most of us will never see an angel with our physical eyes, they are all around us just the same. They always point us to God and want Him alone to be exalted. Angels fly swiftly to carry out God's will in

Breath of God

various situations. Until we reach heaven, we will never know how many times angels have intervened on our behalf. In the next devotion, I have included an angel story. Perhaps you can think of a situation right now when you knew beyond a shadow of a doubt that God had sent an angel to help you.

According to Psalms 91:12, God even notices if we're about to trip on a rock and sends angels to catch us. What a loving God, to assign us bodyguards. In Psalms 103:20, we are told that angels are commissioned when the Word of God is declared. God's angels are on assignment for you. Rejoice.

Prayer:

Thank You, Father, that You left no stone unturned when it came to Your care for us. Today, I want to especially thank You for angels that are on assignment. My family and I are safe in Your arms. I am Your beloved. You are my Shepherd, so I will not walk in fear. Breath of God, come and breathe fresh revelation into my spirit regarding angels and how You use them in my life. Remind me to speak Your Word over every situation. Help me remember angels are near, ready to act on Your Word.

An Angel Story

Luke 4:10 | Psalms 91:9-12

Breath of God, thank You, Father, that there are angels among us.

When my husband was a young man, fresh out of Bible college in 1975, he and a buddy had spent some time working with teens at a Christian ranch in Glasgow, Montana. When camp was over, the young men hopped in Steven's yellow 1967 Plymouth Sport Fury and headed for Minnesota. Unbeknownst to them, the muffler had developed a hole and carbon monoxide was leaking into the cab. As the toxic fumes filled the air, my husband, who was on the passenger side, passed out. His buddy started hallucinating and saw a locomotive coming down the middle of the highway right at them. That's when he realized something was wrong and pulled over onto the side of the road. He passed out before he could shut the car off, so the engine was still running.

As they both lay passed out on the side of the road, my husband heard a woman's voice shouting his name very loudly: "Steven, Steven!" He came to just enough to open the car door. He fell out of the car and rolled into

Breath of God

some chilly water in the ditch. That revived him very quickly. They were in the middle of nowhere and there was nobody around anywhere to be seen. Steven crawled out of the ditch and pulled his buddy out of the vehicle.

By the grace of God, they were safe. The two college buddies drove the rest of the way home with all the windows down. I get chills to this day when my husband shares this story of being rescued by an angel. Thank You, Lord, for sparing my husband's life that day. I am so grateful that there are angels among us.

Prayer:

Oh, what a Father You are! With gentle, tender care You watch over Your children. Your thoughts are ever toward me. On this side of heaven I may never know how many times You sent angels to my side. I have nothing to fear. You are closer than my very breath. I am safe in Your arms.

The Explosive Power of Prayer

John 11:1-44 | James 5:14-16 | Philippians 4:6-7

Breath of God, give me a revelation of the power of prayer.

Dynamic, earthshaking, and explosive. Prayer. It's God's idea. It is His plan in which humanity may humbly connect with deity. What an awesome privilege. All seven billion of us can talk to God at the same time, and He will not miss a beat. The One who placed the sun, moon, and stars in the sky is the One who hears you when you pray. Levels of difficulty do not exist with God. He heals cancer as effortlessly as He soothes a headache. The Bible is filled with miraculous answers to prayer. Each miracle in the Bible is meant to be a faith builder for you.

I believe one of the most profound answers to prayer is found in John 11, where Jesus brings a dead man back to life. Lazarus had been dead four days. His two sisters, Mary and Martha, were devastated over his death. I'm not sure why Jesus waited four whole days before appearing on the scene. Perhaps, in part, it was to ensure there would be no question that their brother Lazarus was not just sleeping. He had no breath in his lungs and no spirit in his body for four days. Lazarus was dead. There would be no denying that what Jesus was about to do would be a miracle.

Jesus told them to remove the stone from Lazarus' tomb. Martha objected that her brother's body would already be decomposing and the smell of rotting flesh would be very offensive. Jesus' answer? "Did I not tell you and promise you that if you would believe and rely on Me, you would see the glory of God?" (John 11:40). At that, they perhaps covered their noses and removed the stone.

Jesus lifted His eyes to Heaven and talked to His Father for a moment. Jesus, our great example, demonstrated a very important life lesson here—to live moment by moment with a heart attitude of dependency and sufficiency on God. We all desperately need our Creator. Without His permission, we cannot even breathe.

Jesus then shouted loudly, "Lazarus, come out!" I believe Jesus said his name so only Lazarus, not the whole graveyard of dead bodies, would come back from the dead. When Jesus speaks into a situation, something dynamic is about to happen. Jesus is in the business of resurrecting dead things back to life. Lazarus came out of his tomb that day. It was resurrection day. Jesus put spirit and breath back into Lazarus' body, turning a funeral into a celebration. Oh, the elation; their brother was back from the dead. What a sweet reunion there must have been. What a miracle.

Prayer:

Oh, Father, thank You for the explosive power of prayer. Thank You that in Your great compassion, You hear me when I call Your name. You are almighty God, and yet You are a personal God. I'm so grateful today that You know my name. Thank You for seeing me and calling my name when I was crawling around in the dungeon of sin. Like Lazarus, You breathed Your breath of life into me when I was among the spiritual walking dead. With loving care, You loosed me from my grave clothes so I could dance. I breathe You in and live. You have delivered me out of the darkness of this world into a life filled with Your light. I am free. I am loved.

Show Me Your Glory

Exodus 33:18-23 | Hebrews 1:3

Breath of God, I want to see You.

In Exodus 33:18, Moses asks God if he may see His glory. God responds by revealing His goodness to Moses. God's goodness must be a very significant part of His nature, for this is what He chose to reveal to Moses.

When we declare, "God is good all the time, and all the time God is good," we are proclaiming a very key facet of His nature. When we cry out for God's glory, we are asking Him to reveal Himself to us. We are asking God that ,as much as our physical body can withstand, "Show me Your glory."

Through all of eternity, there will forever be new dimensions of His glory to discover. As our Father searches throughout the earth, He is pleased to find one who passionately seeks Him with every breath.

Prayer:

Precious heavenly Father, I love Your presence. With holy fear, I'm crying out today for more of

You, for more of Your glory. I want to draw closer to You than ever before. This is my passion.

Thank You that Your glory has not dissipated. The glory You revealed to Moses is the same glory You pour out today upon hungry hearts. May my countenance shine today with the radiance of Your glory.

I wait for You.

The Battlefield

Ephesians 6:10-18 | 2 Corinthians 10:3-5
Isaiah 55:8-12 | Philippians 4:6-9

Breath of God, breathe Your truth, courage, and perseverance into my mind.

They say the mind is a terrible thing to waste. A mind void of God's Word truly is. There is a quote by Albert Einstein that has always stuck with me and made me smile. "I want to know the thoughts of God; the rest are mere details." In these perilous times, possessing the mind of Christ will keep us safely wrapped in God's timeless truth.

The key to victory? Fight. Fight the way Jesus fought. In Matthew 4:1-11 (AMP), Jesus was physically weak after fasting for 40 days, but that did not stop Him from standing firm when the Devil came against Him. Jesus response to each temptation was, "It is written and forever remains written." No matter how weak you feel, breathe out a declaration from the Word of God. Jesus, our great example, showed us how to achieve victory in this area every single time.

Remember Paul's encouraging words from 1 Timothy 6:12, "Fight the good fight of the faith; lay hold of the eternal life to which you were summoned." It will be eternally worth it all.

Prayer:

Father God, Victorious Warrior and Intercessor of my soul, thank You for leading me triumphantly through every battle. You are the Champion of my life, my Hero. Right now, I release control of my mind, will, and emotions to You.

In Jesus' name, I draw a blood-line around my mind. The Devil cannot cross it. I am free from all tormenting thoughts and the shame associated with my past.

I declare that I am love-driven, not performance-driven. I decree that I am rising to new heights each day in my love-walk with God and man. I am being transformed daily from glory to glory into the image of Jesus Christ.

I courageously hold up the shield of faith, which obliterates every flaming thought-missile of the Devil.

I deeply breathe in the mind-transforming truth of God's Holy Word. It is penetrating the deepest part of me, changing me forever. I am more than a conqueror in Jesus' name. Thank You, Father, that I have the mind of Christ.

Breathe His Name

Philippians 2:9-10 | Acts 4:7-12 | Romans 10:13

Breath of God, through it all, I breathe the matchless name of Jesus.

Breathing the name of Jesus invokes His presence, His power, and His authority into any situation. Jesus gives His children the authority to use His name. Jesus loves to hear you whisper His name throughout the day and night. He never sleeps. His name is available every second. Jesus is the Word of God in the flesh. Jesus is the Word, and the Word is full of living power for anything you may be facing today.

As you breathe His name, you welcome Him into the moments of your life, the good times and the hard times. You can rest assured that when the name of Jesus is spoken, He will move heaven and earth to answer your prayer. His name brings peace. His name brings healing. His name brings authority over the Devil. His name is all you will ever need.

Go ahead, say the name of Jesus as many times as you want. He won't become weary of hearing His name. You are the treasure of His heart.

Breath of God

Prayer:

Oh, Jesus, I love Your name. I breathe Your name in worship. I breathe Your name in praise. Your name brings light to the darkness. You came to expose and destroy the works of the Devil. Jesus, I receive Your freedom, peace, healing, joy, wisdom, and authority each time I breathe Your name. Divinely imprint Your Word into the depths my heart so Your Word is what will supernaturally pour out of me in the face of any situation. Holy Spirit, remind me to breathe the name of Jesus always.

It's Your Breath in My Lungs

**John 10:10 | John 3:16 | 1 Peter 3:10-11
Matthew 16:25 | Jeremiah 29:11-14**

Breath of God, I breathe You in and live.

The first step in living the zoe life of God is coming to the realization that we cannot even breathe without His permission. *Surrender* is the key word for breakthrough into the life God has for you. Continued surrender keeps our life in alignment with God's perfect will. It's not the world's way, but it is God's way. Jesus is life.

The breath of God will infuse supernatural life into who you were always meant to be on this planet. It is impossible to experience true life without the breath of God in your lungs.

Those who walk in darkness will be drawn to your light. His light in you will pave the way for eternal life for others also. This is the Good News of the Gospel. Breathe Him in and live.

Breath of God

Prayer:

Gracious Father, I come before You with thanksgiving. You deserve all glory and praise. I am desperate for Your presence. You put the very breath in my lungs. Thank You for giving me life. I want to live the zoe life You have planned for me. Running with my own plans has left me dry and wanting. Pour out Your supernatural springs of refreshing and hope over me. Breathe in me, breath of God.

In Spirit and in Truth

John 4:4-24 | Psalm 145

Breath of God, breathe in me pure worship
to lift up to Your heart.

We are worshiping creatures. Every day, we worship either the Creator or something created. God is love, and in His great love He gives you the power to choose the object of your affection. How He longs for you to choose Him, but He will not demand your worship.

God searches the earth for lovers—imperfect, surrendered, passionate lovers—who choose Him above all else. His ears, His eyes, and His heart are drawn to those whose magnificent obsession is Him alone. He alone is God. He alone is worthy of your worship.

You were born for this!

Prayer:

Holy God, as You search the earth for a true worshiper this day, may Your ears be drawn this way. May my praises rise like incense to the chambers of Your heart. You are my desire. You are the object of my praise. I choose to worship You.

I hear the clarion call to join true worshipers from all over the world. May my offering of worship be mingled with theirs. Let the sound of passionate worship resound through all of heaven and earth to You, the One true God.

Fresh Bread from Heaven

Deuteronomy 8:3 | Psalm 16
Matthew 4:4 | John 6:48-51

Breath of God, feed me today with fresh bread from heaven.

Ah, the aroma of fresh bread. There's nothing quite like it. I will never forget as a child coming home from school to the smell of freshly baked bread. When my brothers and sisters and I were growing up, it was Mom's tradition to bake bread each week. Even before we entered the house, the aroma would draw us in. Oh, the anticipation of indulging in one of our tastiest after-school treats. Mom would slice some for us while it was still warm. We'd smother it with butter and jam and, with much elation, partake.

John 21:4-13 tells us that one morning Jesus prepared breakfast for His disciples. On the menu was fresh bread and fish. Jesus' disciples had fished all night and caught nothing. They got "skunked," as we say in Minnesota. Any fisherman can understand how disappointing that must have been. Jesus could feel their disappointment and called out to them to cast their nets on the other side of the boat. When they did, their nets were so full of fish—153 to be exact—they could hardly haul them in. The disciples found out once again that good things happened when they listened and obeyed the Master.

After a long, grueling night, I'm sure they were very hungry and weary. The aroma of fresh bread and fried fish filled the country morning air as the disciples approached the shore line of the Sea of Galilee. I can picture them scurrying a little faster as they inhaled the scrumptious fragrance. Jesus called out to them to come and join Him. I'm sure they all accepted His invitation.

I really enjoy envisioning the morning Jesus cooked breakfast for His disciples. In John 6:51, Jesus describes Himself as the "Bread that came down from heaven." In Matthew 4:4, Jesus says, "Man shall not live and be upheld and sustained by bread alone, but by every word that comes forth from the mouth of God." And again, in John 6:48, Jesus describes Himself as "the Bread of Life [that gives life—the Living Bread]." I can just imagine the laughter and rich conversation that took place as they ate together and then lingered afterward around the fire. Have you ever painted a picture in your mind of Jesus laughing? How I would have loved to be there as Jesus, the Bread of Life, ministered fresh manna to the souls of those fishermen that day.

Today, Jesus still calls. He invites all of humanity to come and dine at His table. On the menu? Fresh heavenly Bread that is out of this world. Listen to His voice as

He beckons, "Come, My child, come and eat to your heart's content."

Prayer:

Jesus, Bread of heaven, the rich aroma of Your presence is a continual feast. I truly live as Your Word is breathed into my spirit. The Bread of Your presence nourishes and satisfies me completely. It is here with You that I lack for nothing. Every morsel of Your Word and Your presence is a delightful feast to my spirit.

As my to-do list lengthens by the moment, help me to stay here. Help me live so close to You that I can hear Your heart beating and Your holy breath upon me. Feed me, I pray, with fresh manna from heaven as I wait for You.

God Dances over You

Zephaniah 3:17 | Mark 12:30

Breath of God, breathe within me a vision of
You dancing over me.

The Jerusalem Bible version of Zephaniah 3:17 says, "Yahweh your God is there with you, the warrior-Savior. He will rejoice over you with happy song, He will dance with shouts of joy for you." Have you ever pictured your heavenly Father rejoicing over you to the point that He breaks into dancing?

How do you picture God? Do you see Him as the "All-Seeing Eye" kind of Father, critical and quick to punish? I am so glad this verse is in the Bible. It is delightful to envision our heavenly Father dancing over His children. God's Word tells us what delights His heart. Just as a child longs to please their earthly father, we are to find great delight in pleasing our Father in heaven.

Today, I believe God wants to breathe a fresh vision into your spirit of how He truly feels about you as His cherished son or daughter. Awakening to this truth will carry you and motivate you with deeper passion to fight the good fight of faith and run with God's divine call on your life.

Breath of God

Envision the God of the universe dancing over you today.

Prayer:

Oh, Father, today I pray that high praises will flow freely from my heart to Your very throne room. Create the fruit of my lips as I worship You. I adore You. In the deepest part of me, I long to please You. I want to bring such joy to Your heart that You dance over me. Wrap me in Your arms so I can join You in a divine dance. Help me go through this day enveloped in Your favor, covered with the kisses of heaven.

Heavenly Father, may I have this dance?

Beauty for Ashes

Isaiah 61:1-7 | Ecclesiastes 3:11
Psalms 51:1-12 | Jeremiah 29:11-14

Breath of God, thank You, Father, for exchanging the ashes of my life with Your beauty.

I forgive you. Your past is forgotten. I threw it all into the bottom of the deepest sea, never to be remembered again. I forgive you, My child. I forgive you." The moment of that pronouncement from Jesus, the fresh air of heaven blows into your heart and you can live again. Jesus lovingly breathes these healing words to those broken with sorrow over their sin. They are like flowers of hope on which the master gardener, Jesus, inscribes on each blossom, "Forgiven."

That is the power of the cross. That is the power in the blood of Jesus. Sin does not have to carry the final word in your life. Jesus' sacrifice is the breath of hope for all of humanity.

God's love and forgiveness releases you from the ashes of your past. Breathe in the beauty of this revelation. Dignity, peace, and joy are the treasured gifts of the forgiven.

Prayer:

Oh, Father, I am so thankful today that You have replaced the ashes of my life with beauty. Though my past was filled with failure and disappointment, my future is bright with Your living hope.

Because of You, my past does not define me. Thank You that I walk each day as a forgiven, beloved child of God. No more ashes of shame and guilt remain. I am now defined only by who You say I am.

Every word curse that has been spoken over my life is cut off in Jesus' name. Nothing can hold me back from experiencing Your presence and Your destiny for my life. Because I've been forgiven, I walk with a gracious, compassionate heart toward others. May my life exude the joy and peace of a forgiven child of God.

Thank You, Father. Because of You, my life is beautiful.

Fresh Oil

Exodus 30:22-33 | 1 Samuel 16
Hebrews 1:8-9 | Matthew 25:4

Breath of Heaven, saturate me today with
Your fresh oil.

When a rose is crushed, the oil in each petal releases a very beautiful fragrance. I believe this is a picture of a true follower of Christ. Like a rose, when we are crushed by the circumstances of life the sweet aroma of the Holy Spirit is released. How beautiful is the fragrance of a life surrendered to God.

Oil is one of the symbols of the Holy Spirit used in Scripture. In Exodus 30, God revealed to Moses a special recipe for the sacred holy anointing oil. Below is a list of the ingredients, along with a basic spiritual meaning for us today:

- Myrrh symbolizes a true disciple of Jesus who delights in obedience to Him and is dead to the things of this world.

- Sweet cinnamon signifies standing upright with integrity in this corrupt world.

- Sweet calamus signifies growth even in difficult places as we draw our strength and nourishment from the Vine, Jesus.
- Cassia represents reverence and bowing down in worship.
- Olive oil represents the binding of all the other oils together—the carrier oil, so to speak—promoting unity in the body of Christ.

Jesus' deep love for humanity constrained Him to be crushed with the weight of the world's sin. Jesus endured the whip and the nails to buy our pardon and healing. God uses the crushing trials of life that we may exude the fragrance of His Son to the world. When the world encounters you, may they encounter the fragrant oil of the One who dwells in you.

Prayer:

Precious Holy Spirit, saturate me today with a fresh release of Your anointing oil. More and more of You is my heart's desire. Pour Your oil over me again and again as I go through this day. Supernaturally guide my steps so I make it to every appointment orchestrated by Your hand. Help me to listen to Your still, small voice and to block out the distracting noise of this world. Give me Your eyes to see what I otherwise would be blind to. Grant me wisdom and discernment so I may be instant in season and out of season with a word, a prayer, a smile, or a touch for those You place in my path today.

Supernatural Provision

1 Kings 17:7-16 | Philippians 4:19
Matthew 6:25-34 | Psalm 23

Breath of God, You are my Provider.

It is so easy to get into the trap of believing that our job, the work of our own hands, is our provider. This lie from the enemy can leave us feeling either pressured and overwhelmed or prideful. It is God who gives us physical strength and the power to gain wealth. He is the source of our very breath. Just as God provided manna in the desert for the Israelites, He will provide for you. Do not fear, God will rain down manna again should the need arise. God's children will never lack for any good thing.

May the story below be a beautiful reminder of the fact that God is your provider. Let it lift the pressure that causes you to believe that it's all up to you if your bills will be paid and food will be on the table.

God told Elijah in 1 Kings 17 to travel to a widow's home in Zarephath, for she would provide food for him. There was a famine in the land, so food was scarce. When Elijah arrived at the gate of the city, there was the woman gathering sticks. He called to the woman requesting some water. Now, that was not such a difficult request, but as she was going to get it, Elijah called to her again asking for a morsel of bread. Elijah did not realize that this poor widow was gathering sticks so she could prepare her last meal for herself and her son. The flour and oil jars would soon be empty and they would die of starvation, or so they thought.

I can just imagine how her heart sank at this request. But God was about to make a way where there seemed to be no way. With faith mixed with a little fear, I'm sure, the widow offered her last meal to the prophet. Just as God promised, her flour and oil jars never went empty. I can just imagine the joy and wonderment that would fill their eyes each morning as they gazed into the pots to find God's provision before their very eyes. Jesus never fails.

Prayer:

Precious Father, You are my Provider. Thank You for knowing my every need before I ask. I rejoice that my life is safe in Your hands. I fear nothing at all because You are with me. Reveal to me a seed, a gift that I can share with someone, that I may be a blessing in their life. I confess that my job is not my provider; You are, Father. I find peace in Your name, Jehovah-Jireh, my Provider. I hold

Your name ever so close to my heart. Jesus, You never fail. You cannot fail. Today, I rest in Your unfailing love and divine provision.

The Master Goldsmith

1 Corinthians 9:24 | Philippians 3:14 | 3 John 4

Breath of God, may You behold Your reflection in me.

Through the years, we've observed with a smile our little grandchildren as they closely watch us and, with childlike enthusiasm, attempt to imitate our every move. Their innocent little eyes admire the adults in their lives, and they aspire to become just like us.

Children aren't the only ones who are growing up. From the moment we become a child of God, the journey begins of becoming more and more like Him. Just like a child, we desire to be like our heavenly Father.

I have heard that our spiritual journey can be compared to the old-fashioned way of refining gold. In this process, the goldsmith would turn up the temperature of the fire to 1,064 degrees or more. The extremely high temperature would cause the gold to melt, and impurities would rise to the top. Layer by layer, the goldsmith would carefully remove anything that was not pure, 100 percent gold. The purifying process continued until, as the goldsmith gazed into the pot, he could clearly see his own reflection looking back at him.

Breath of God

Our heavenly Father is the master goldsmith, lovingly refining us into His image.

Prayer:

Loving Father, thank You for hand-picking me out of the darkness of this world. I am so grateful that You rescued me. I love walking in Your light. Though Your refining fire burns hot, it's worth it all. When You gaze into the refining pot of my life, may I shine like pure gold and bring a smile to Your face. I say, "Yes, Lord. Make me and mold me. "

Hear the cry of my heart today, "More of You, Jesus, less of me."

God-Breathed Dreams

Joel 2:28 | Matthew 2:13 | Acts 2:17-18

Breath of God, speak to me through my dreams.

Does God speak through dreams today? Our minds can get so cluttered and distracted during the day with all the business of life. As we sleep, our subconscious mind and our spirit are at rest and open for God to speak to us through divinely granted dreams. We are spirit beings. God speaks Spirit to spirit.

In the Bible, God used dreams many times to communicate important messages and warnings. The prophet Joel prophesied that in the last days God would give His people dreams and visions. Although we must always ensure they line up with God's Word, dreams are one of the ways God can speak to us.

Before you go to sleep, ask God to guard your dreams and give you dreams from His heart. Ask the Holy Spirit to speak to you through them. Keep a notebook and pen by your bed. If you have a dream that seems significant, ask the Holy Spirit for wisdom and discernment and share it with a mature brother or sister in Christ.

Prayer:

Precious Holy Spirit, You are the perfect teacher and guide. You are my ever-present help in times of trouble. Thank You for guiding me into all truth through Your Word. I trust You, Lord, to direct my journey step by step until I fulfill the purpose for which I was created. Forgive me for allowing myself to become so busy that I miss Your voice.

As I sleep, use dreams to speak to me. Help me to pay attention and obey. Please impart wisdom, discernment, and clarity as I seek what You would say to me through my dreams. I pray Your kingdom come and Your will be done in me. Speak, Lord. I am listening.

Inhale, Exhale

Psalms 139:1-18 | Psalm 150

Breath of God, You are the air I breathe.

Inhale, exhale, inhale, exhale. You naturally do this twenty-four hours a day, up to 30,000 times each day, without even consciously thinking about it. The way God formed your body to function is so magnificent. Even as you sleep, your body automatically knows to inhale oxygen and exhale carbon dioxide. Your Creator fashioned you with such intricacy, wisdom, and love.

Just as your physical body needs oxygen to survive, your spirit needs the breath of God. Without the breath of God, we experience, at best, a shallow existence on this earth. Jesus said, "I am the way, the truth, and the life." No Jesus, no life.

The realization of our deep dependence upon God for our very breath is humbling, as it should be. It is reason to give Him all of our praise as long as we have breath.

Inhale deeply of His presence today and live, truly live.

Prayer:

Gracious Father, giver of the very breath I breathe, I worship You. I lift my hands and rejoice at the wonder of my birth. I give honor this day to whom honor is due. You own it all. Your hands made it all. Your voice thunders throughout the universe, "I Am!"

You wanted me to be. You gave me breath to praise You and know You intimately. You deserve all my worship. I give myself to You, loving Father. May my life be a praise to Your heart. May how I live my life bring a smile to Your face, dear Father.

Our Eternal Home

**John 14:1-6 | Hebrews 11:8-10
2 Corinthians 5:1-10**

Breath of God, You are the mansion builder.

Home. Most of us can hardly wait to get back home after a long day. Our family is there, our most comfortable chair, and our bed. It's the place where we can take off our shoes, relax, and find refreshment away from the chaos of the outside world. Yes, there's no place like home.

When Jesus walked on the earth, He was a builder. He learned the trade of carpentry from His earthly father, Joseph. He grew up listening to the sounds of sawing, pounding of nails, and the clapping of wood. I'm sure Jesus smiled as He humbly watched and learned the trade, even though He may have already known everything there was to know on the subject.

In obedience, Jesus left the glory of heaven to rescue you and me from the darkness and penalty of sin. After He fulfilled His mission on earth, Jesus went back home to His heavenly Father.

Jesus is there now, praying for us and building mansions. They are beautiful mansions that will never require

Breath of God

repair. Jesus is the mansion-builder. If you're not already on it, Jesus longs to add you to His mansion-building list.

Eternity lasts forever. Breathe each moment with your heart set on eternity.

Prayer:

Dear Jesus, I'm home when I'm with You. I love Your presence. I bring an offering of worship to You, my King. You are the master builder. Thank You for the promise in Your Word that You are building a mansion for me. You know my favorite colors and style. You know what will bring joy and delight to my heart.

You are such a loving Father. It is an honor to belong to Your family. I was born to be with You forever. Keep me in the palm of Your hand all the days of my life until I see You face to face and enter my eternal home in heaven.

Closer

Psalms 16:11 | Psalm 51
Isaiah 66:2 | Proverbs 18:24

Breath of God, I hear You drawing me closer.

"Come closer," Jesus calls. "I want to be with you. I want you to see Me. I want you to know Me. Like Adam, I formed you and put breath in you so we could have a close, intimate friendship forever.

"When you feel an awkward distance between us, a humble, repentant heart opens the door wide for restored intimacy between us.

"Enter My presence with thanksgiving. Fathers like to be appreciated, you know. I knew what I was doing when I formed you in your mother's womb. I saw to it that each unique quality you possess was stamped with My fingerprints.

"Although I already know your every thought, I am blessed when you share everything with Me. There is no subject that is taboo between us. You are safe with Me. Although I am God and have need of nothing, I long to be close to you because I love you.

Breath of God

"Nothing in this world can satisfy like the bread of My presence. It is a continual feast.

"I am close to the humble of heart. I am close to those who tremble at My Word.

"Come, My child, and sit for a while."

Prayer:

I hear You calling, Jesus, and I am coming. Your voice draws me like sweet music. I approach You and see Your arms open wide to receive me. You invite me to climb up on Your lap and rest in Your warm embrace. I want to stay here forever, Father. I am listening, anticipating each beat of Your heart.

The bread of Your presence is a gourmet meal to my soul. I am satisfied.

You are my very best Friend, the One with whom I share the deepest secrets of my heart.

There is no place I would rather be, no place at all, than with You.

Breathe in His Word

**Hebrews 4:12-13 | Proverbs 18:21
Psalms 71:8 | Psalms 19:4**

Breath of God, I inhale and exhale Your living Word today.

God's Word is alive. There are millions of books out there calling for your attention. There is only one Book whose every word is alive and full of power—God's Word. As you feed upon the words in the Bible, you fill your spirit with the life-giving bread of heaven. It nourishes and breathes supernatural life into you. It gives you discernment over all the voices out there shouting your name.

Even though your natural mind may not understand it all, you are still feeding your spirit with the bread of His presence. The humble act of feeding on God's Word ignites the power of God in your life. The Holy Spirit takes that Word and builds you up and infuses God's divine wisdom inside of you.

His Word is life. Inhale God's Word so you can exhale His Word into the atmosphere. His Word causes His kingdom to come and His will to be done in you. Your

Breath of God

God-ordained destiny is wrapped in the pages of His Word. Breathe in the Word of God and live.

Prayer:

Dear heavenly Father, I ask today for an insatiable hunger for Your Word. Let each word come alive in my spirit and strengthen me to follow You. Help me to hide Your Word in my heart so I can resist sin. May Your Word grow deep roots in the soil of my heart.

Thank You that the Devil runs in terror at the sound of Your Word coming out of my mouth. I'm so grateful for Your Word, for Your holy roadmap for living.

Holy Spirit, please help me to retain and memorize Your Word. I believe and receive Your living Word into my spirit.

Your Word is a lamp unto my feet and a light guiding my path. Let my light shine brightly because of Your living Word within me.

The Names of God

1 John 4:9-16 | Romans 5:8

Breath of God, thank You for the power in Your name.

God has a name or attribute to meet every situation and need we may encounter in this fallen world. Nothing is too difficult for Him. Nothing surprises Him. Nothing worries Him.

What do you need God to be in your life today? Tell Him. Meditate on His names and speak them out loud. Allow the Lord to bring revelation of His mighty power to fulfill those in your life.

His name will lift you high above any circumstance you may be facing. The truth in His name will lead you out of any area of defeat into the place of triumph that Jesus said belongs to you as His beloved child.

God, You are my:

Father, Rock, Breath Giver, Best Friend, King, Mansion Builder, Burden Bearer, Healer of all things, Great I Am, Champion, Master Artist, Defender, Lawyer, Debt Payer, Sacrifice, Hero, Merciful Lord, Protector, Holy God, Author and Completer of my faith, Righteous

Breath of God

Judge, Leader into All Truth, Strength, Righteousness, Banner, Creator, Discerner, Pardon, Wisdom, Spiritual Gift Giver, Freedom, Deliverer, Greatest Treasure, All-Sufficient One, Reward, All Knowing One, Ever Present One, All Powerful One, Maker of the Stars, Miracle Worker, Life Sustainer, Wisdom, Restorer, Reconciler, Advocate, Stand By, Liberator, Lord, Master, Sanctifier, Victorious One, Resurrected King, Lover of My Soul, History Maker, Emanuel, Provider, Hope, Salvation, Conquering King, Sovereign Lord, Life, All in All, Inspiration, my Peace, my Joy, Soon Coming King.

Today Lord, I need You to be my:

_____
_____
_____
_____
_____
_____

Prayer:

Thank You, Father God, that I am the recipient of Your great love. Thank You for taking such loving care of me, my family, and all that concerns me. You're a good, good Father. You're my perfect Father. You're my life, my joy, and my peace. You put breath in my lungs to declare

Your Word and praise You. Thank You for breath. Let Your Word come alive in me today. Remind me, Holy Spirit, to breathe Your name over every situation I face. I love Your Word. Help me to be a reflection of Your Word inside of me.

With love, _____

The Main Thing

Ecclesiastes 12:9-14 | Isaiah 26:3
Isaiah 66:1-2 | Psalms 119:1-7

Breath of God, help me keep the main thing,
the main thing.

There are a multitude of voices and opinions out there shouting for you to believe them. Knowledge on any subject imaginable is at the tip of our fingers. God's Word is truth. Hone in on what God says is important. Focusing your thoughts on Him will free your mind of false beliefs and clutter. It will eliminate chaos and fill you with supernatural peace.

King Solomon summed it all up with this timeless truth, "fear God…and keep His commandments" (Ecclesiastes 12:13). The fear of the Lord is having a heart that cringes at the thought of hurting or offending Him.

From the beginning, we were designed to honor our Maker and be best friends with Him. The consequences of neglecting the main thing are sadly evident all around us.

Your heavenly Father knows what is best. He knows everything. He knows you and loves you deeply. Fill your mind with the Father's life-giving Word.

Breath of God

Breathe Him in and watch the clutter and chaos fly away.

Prayer:

Dear heavenly Father, You are the uncreated One. You are the almighty God. I worship You. I trust You. I fix my eyes on You. You are the author and completer of my faith. Help me today to keep the main thing, the main thing. Forgive me, Father, for making You so small in my eyes. Give me a vision of Your greatness so the things of this world will become small. Be magnified.

Thank You that when I was wallowing around in the dark chaos of this world, You saw me, You loved me, and You rescued me. Your presence is my vital need.

Help me today to keep the main thing, the main thing. Come, I pray, and breathe Your breath of life into me. Refresh me with the sweet wind of Your Holy Spirit.

Dry Bones Come Alive

Ezekiel 37:1-14 | Isaiah 40:29-31

Breath of God, breathe Your life into the dry bones.

In the breath of God is the breath of life, both spiritually and physically. Nothing is impossible with God. No one is so hopeless that the breath of God cannot raise them to life. No addiction has more power than the life-giving breath of God. No trial or tribulation has more power than the breath of God. There is power in the name of Jesus. There is power in His blood. He is the conquering King of kings and Lord of lords. God is sovereign. Jesus' victory at the cross sealed your hope.

God is in the business of raising dead things to life. Ask Him today to breathe His breath of life into any circumstance that feels hopeless or dead in your life. Tell those dry bones, "Live, in Jesus' name." Hallelujah! He reigns.

Breath of God

Prayer:

Holy Father, thank You for breathing Your breath of life into me. Thank You for raising me up from the bed of spiritual death and hopelessness. You are the life-giver. I breathe in Your life, giving breath today over every circumstance in my life. Circumstances will not defeat me. Because of You, I will run and not grow weary. I will walk and not faint. I mount up on wings like the eagle and soar closer and closer to the source of my life. Because You live, Jesus, I live.

Jesus' Final Breath

John 19:30 | Revelation 12:7-11
Colossians 2:15 | 1 Corinthians 15:54-57

Breath of God, Your final breath sealed my victory forever.

Death by crucifixion was excruciating. Each breath was a fight to take in and release. Jesus could have easily summoned thousands of angels to rescue him. He could have jumped off that cross Himself, but He didn't. The most important assignment in all of history had to be accomplished or there would be no hope for you or for me. Mankind desperately needed a hero. This ultimate display of sacrifice and love would pave the way for our reconciliation to the Father.

It surely looked like a victory for the Devil. Cheers from the crowd and the hordes of hell filled Jesus' ears, but He was not moved. Jesus' eyes were focused on something—you. He lovingly endured the cross for you. A huge awakening and defeat was in store for the Devil. The most massive victory of all time was about to rock hell and the whole earth.

In agony, Jesus shouted one final sentence, *"It is finished!"* And it was.

Jesus went to hell for us and stole the keys of death, hell, and the grave away from the Devil. On the third day, He rose from the dead. Jesus lives. Jesus is alive forevermore.

Prayer:

Oh, Jesus, I want to thank You with all my heart that you completed Your mission on earth. You obeyed Your Father until absolute victory was achieved.

"Thank You" just doesn't seem to be enough. It doesn't begin to express what I feel in my heart for all You have done. Your love is so amazing. While I was a wretched sinner, You saw me through eyes of love. You saw what I could be. You hung on the cross for me.

You took this selfish, prideful sinner and flooded me with forgiveness, freedom, and light. I could never thank You enough. You have my heart forever. I'm completely ruined for this world and completely captivated by Your love. I am eternally alive in You. Help me never forget that I have been bought with a price.

My blessed hope awaits—eternity with You.

It is finished!

About the Author

Joni Banks has been a follower of the Lord Jesus for more than fifty years. She and her husband, Steven, serve the Lord through a home ministry called Fountain of Hope where they emphasize the Word, servanthood, intercession, and worship. Joni finds joy in leading people to the throne through praise and intimate worship and has a deep desire for everyone to experience the love of God. Her first identity is as a beloved, forgiven daughter of King Jesus. Joni is blessed to enjoy life with her best friend and husband, Steven, and their wonderful children and grandchildren.

Joni can be contacted at jworshippers@aol.com.

5 FOLD MEDIA

We are a Christian-based publishing company that was founded in 2009. Our primary focus has been to establish authors.

"5 Fold Media was the launching partner that I needed to bring *The Transformed Life* into reality. This team worked diligently and with integrity to help me bring my words and vision into manifestation through a book that I am proud of and continues to help people and churches around the world. None of this would have been possible without the partnership and education I received from 5 Fold Media."

- Pastor John Carter, Lead Pastor of Abundant Life Christian Center, Syracuse, NY, Author and Fox News Contributor

*The Transformed Life is foreworded by Pastor A.R. Bernard, received endorsements from best-selling authors Phil Cooke, Rick Renner, and Tony Cooke, and has been featured on television shows such as TBN and local networks.

5 Fold Media

5701 E. Circle Dr. #338, Cicero, NY 13039

manuscript@5foldmedia.com

Find us on Facebook, Twitter, and YouTube.

Discover more at www.5FoldMedia.com.

CPSIA information can be obtained
at www.ICGtesting.com
Printed in the USA
BVHW05s1459030818
523344BV00006B/98/P

9 781942 056652